The Broken World

To Jim —
thank you for your
efforts to *heal* the
broken people of this
world. Love ♡
Beth & Al ♪
2003

The
Broken
World

Poems by
Marcus Cafagña

University of Illinois Press   Urbana and Chicago

This book is printed on acid-free paper.

Library of Congress Cataloging-in-Publication Data

Cafagña, Marcus.
    The broken world : poems / by Marcus Cafagña.
        p.   cm. — (The National Poetry series)
    ISBN 0-252-06550-6 (alk. paper)
    I. Title. II. Series.
PS3553.A317B76   1996
811'.54—dc20   95-41769
                                      CIP

Acknowledgments

I wish to thank the editors of the following publications in which these poems originally appeared (sometimes in altered form) or are forthcoming:

Agni: "Something Faithful," "The Way He Breaks"
Borderlands: Texas Poetry Review: "*Chingada*" (under the title "Eastern High: 1967")
The Burning World: "The House on Lyons Avenue"
The Capital Times: "Back in the World"
Cincinnati Poetry Review: "Cracking Eggs"
Harvard Review: "Justice," "Modigliani: *Venus Naturalis*"
The Iowa Review: "Remission"
The Kenyon Review: "The Broken World"
Negative Capability: "Mammography"
Ploughshares: "Little Girl in Blue, 1918"
Poetry: "Dybbuks"
The Quarterly: "Feeding," "Psoriasis"
River Rat Review: "Hawthorne Metal, Detroit, 1939"
Seneca Review: "Black Girl on the Overpass"
Sky: "Geography"
The Threepenny Review: "My Aunt Calls from Bellevue"
Tikkun: "Aunt Sarah (1903–81)"
Witness: "All the Bells"

"The American Dream" appears in *Elvis in a Box,* compiled by Robert Turney (East Lansing, Mich.: Privately published, 1992); "Dybbuks," in *Muses,* a publication of the College of Arts and Letters, Michigan State University (East Lansing, 1993); and "Something Faithful" and "The Way He Breaks," in *On the Verge: Emerging Poets and Artists,* edited by Thomas Sayers Ellis and Joseph Lease (Boston: Agni Review with Faber and Faber, 1993).

Some background information and imagery in "Little Girl in Blue, 1918" and "Modigliani: *Venus Naturalis*" are derived from Carol Mann, *Modigliani* (New York: Thames and Hudson, 1980).

I want to express gratitude to my family and, for their help, to William Barillas, Andrea Hollander Budy, Dianne Cafagña, Nancy Vieira Couto, Eric Crosley, Jim Daniels, Peter Marcus, Sharon Olds, Mike Shelton, Gary Soto, Diane Wakoski, and a special thanks to Marc J. Sheehan.

The National Poetry Series

The National Poetry Series was established in 1978 to publish five collections of poetry annually through five participating publishers. The manuscripts are selected by five poets of national reputation. Publication is funded by James A. Michener, The Copernicus Society of America, Edward J. Piszek, The Lannan Foundation, The National Endowment for the Arts, and the Tiny Tiger Foundation.

1995 Competition Winners

Heather Allen, *Leaving a Shadow*
Selected by Denise Levertov, published by
Copper Canyon Press

Marcus Cafagña, *The Broken World*
Selected by Yusef Komunyakaa, published by the
University of Illinois Press

Daniel Hall, *Strange Relation*
Selected by Mark Doty, published by
Viking Penguin Press

Juliana Spahr, *Response*
Selected by Lyn Hejinian, published by
Sun & Moon Press

Karen Volkman, *Crash's Law*
Selected by Heather McHugh, published by
W. W. Norton

For Noelle

He was happy and, so far, lucky—he knew that. His parents were still living, his brothers and his sister were established, his friends from college had gone out to take their places in the world. So far, he had kept away from any real harm, from those forces he knew existed and that could cripple or bring down a man if the luck went bad, if things suddenly turned.

—*Raymond Carver, "A Small, Good Thing"*

Contents

The Broken World is imbued with a beguiling clarity that distills fragmented moments and attempts to connect them. Each poem is a facet of psychological and emotional complexity that approximates our modern lives, invoking a collective seamlessness. There's a simplicity here that instructs and informs, without being mundane and predictable; the imagery takes us through a tough, toe-to-toe dance of textures and tensions. This tabulation of broken things (beings) tells us what we must know and confront in order to make ourselves whole in the modern world. It has everything to do with surviving through a truth that humanizes. The hard facts are held together by lyrical, imaginative detours that accrue into an impressive tour de force. A reverence for the small blessings our lives are made of is what holds *The Broken World* together.

—*Yusef Komunyakaa*

The Way He Breaks

When I separate the blinds today
I watch the dark-haired kid
across the street, shooting baskets
hard with both hands. He's had it
with the Crisis Center. The aluminum
backboard shudders each attempt,
the ball most often rolling the rim
but not dropping through. He's pounded
rubber over cement too many days,
over battered painted foul lines,
dribbled and faked his way between
imaginary defenders. No one there
when he finally makes the shot.
What holds him to this place?
What act of bad luck?
Who might he miss when suddenly he
pauses, frozen in Olympic posture,
focused on the hoop, the missing net,
as if something has just occurred
inside him that makes all of this
some kind of rotten joke? The way
he breaks from that—sprints
into the highest jump
like someone drowning,
pushing his weight
up off the bottom.

Hoods

That's why we cut class
to huddle in parked cars, angora sweaters
chafing at flesh. Phil vainly sculpting
a blonde wave across his forehead
while I aimed someone's rearview.
How girls wearing pinafores
and Peter Pan collars smirked, afraid
of lake wind snarling their curls
down a backseat or up our shirts.
What we studied was the curve of skirt
on some doll fresh from reform school
as she straddled her boyfriend's bike.
We couldn't light anything more than her
cigarette, knew she saw through us
the way a white blouse shows
its black bra, that once I matched
my shame against her boredom, she'd snap
her gum and tease with easy swagger
or shove me on a fender, sharpened nails
pinching deep within my pockets.
What she left were shadows, hair
zipping behind her like a black flag,
that laugh rich and harsh as a Harley's torque,
as if any place she went was hers.

The House on Lyons Avenue

Those mornings on Lyons Avenue,
Linda Taylor puffed Kools
in her mother's living room
and passed out cold beer, while you
and Sharon and Mary all ratted
and sprayed your hair, lined eyes
dark as hers, squeezed Bombshell Pink
with 79¢ lipsticks stolen
from Van Peenan's.
                              Nights, Vic
swung the motorcycle like
a flashlight over the unlit porch,
rose up in his leather jacket
and combed back the wave
only Linda could touch, so sexy
in her white pants you swooned
to think of hands pinning wrists,
unbuttoning that blouse, every torture
his fingers must try.
                              You knew
he'd ruin her outfit, heard
how men under her passion came
long before they could unsnap
her pants, how in that house
decorated with beach towels
and Kewpie dolls won at carnivals,
no one had a chance.

Chingada

for Carol Morris

At sunrise Olivia Cortez
plucked eyebrows against a bathroom mirror
and kissed rings of smoke
toward the ceiling, a small letting out
not for Elias her brother
in prison but Gloria
her friend, whose hair she ratted
for an hour, leaving on a sink
the comb none of us
dared to touch.

Olivia dressed in hip-stitched skirts
for her *pachuco*
because he'd scratched their legend
on high school walls. She was always
last up the steps hissing curses
after our teacher Doug Clark,
stifling as his after-shave,
who wagered she'd fail.

I saw the hurt dilate
her eyes, the unknown side
she'd one day call *chingada*
in a voice so low it unleashed her breath,
her red smear of lipstick,
her stiletto,
how I hadn't yet begun to *toughen up*
until squeezed back in the corner
where the words he spit
rattled and shut her in
as he thrust past us.

I found the little purse
beneath the bleachers: two tampons,
a half pack of Luckies,
the pearl-handled knife.
Unprepared I've opened
myself like the catch
that springs the blade.

Black Girl on the Overpass

wants no more bars around her, not even
the wire mesh her face has pressed,
rusty crosshatch of anger
that indents her forehead. The lack
of fear that has just recently
fenced her in, seized her skin
with metal, puffed raw as Daddy's
before it burst. We'd hardly know it:
our noisy cars bypassing all the signs
to Detroit, people who jump
from heights like this. We approach
and she hurls a ball off the bridge
that suddenly catches wind and unfurls
wings red as a cardinal. And it's her
bandanna somersaulting six lanes
of exhaust, flag of a forgotten
country tossed like a life
to the horizon in the rearview,
shrinking her colors
out of sight.

Something Faithful

I can't imagine the seasons
of ruffles and turtlenecks until she
allowed it to be seen,

my Aunt Eleanor's throat scarred
by the blade of a knife.
But now it's the itch of healing

at family gatherings. In something
low cut the scar is a deep red
valley into which I cannot

look. Still she's never accused
my cousin of madness or hated
the heroin he tried to kick

with Quaaludes. She only ducks
her chin at times, says
it shows a mother and son

can live separate
lives since a scar is something
faithful, a way her skin

will never give him up.

Justice

Why, this afternoon, does the monkey's
hairless jaw when it flicks out saliva
dripping along her arm, and a husband's
dagger-tongued laughter sweeping from
the porch outside to needle and pin her
to the cloth of other men's bad jokes,
their spiky shadows crisscross
at her window? And when later
the monkey's screeching so shrill that
the burglar mask and nostrils flare
in anguish, so like her husband's
before each drunken rage; will the long
greasy fingers try to grip hers
again through the bars of a cage,
though she wriggles from the grasp,
another Roman in his helmet: her shock
of hair like the Sabine women,
their mouths wounded open, she wonders
where justice is, that divine Madonna
mourning a boy on her lap and marriage
vows rolled away; but now the beast
with his prehensile fist pounds
at her, pounds at her to turn
the deadbolt, and as she tries
frantically to escape from the second
story down a ladder and trips on rungs,
clutching her ears from the monkey's
wild screams that her husband

is creeping back around the house,
that justice is around the corner
right behind her, rushing
and rushing through the yard.

Psoriasis

The burning record of the body for those
who know how to read it. I saw the fear
of being rise on bleeding hills of skin.
This is how I began to separate from myself,
the endless sheets of mica I collected
as a boy, transparencies of the rock.
I know I will always give myself
to this woman, the goldenseal salve
coming off on my fingers
like leaves, an eventual new skin.

Remission

Walking home up the many flights after chemo,
the harshly lit little room.
Dark yellow grain of wallpaper
gleaming in the streetlight like stained wood.
The silhouette of a face stares back from the window.
I remember wet, green Pennsylvania mountains.
The other patients in the bathroom
with me, toking joints for depression.
The doctors breaking skin for a good vein.
Or wading the edge of water
at Socorro. Still a teenager joyriding
with Angel Salazar through the state
of New Mexico. With a retooled Chevy
across the desert after dark.
Parking it later where the Rio Grande narrows,
both of us lounging on the hood.
How I envied his cool detachment,
his pidgin breaking with bottles
of beer. A string of bubbles
floating up the neck, those two rubber prophets
poised above the dash,
as if about to come to life.

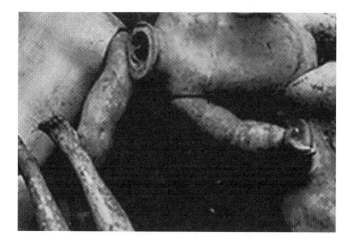

This Rapture

for Cherelyn

Before today my body was useless.
—Anne Sexton, "The Kiss"

         When you curl
against me naked, sideways
and backward on the bed
spooned together, tangled
within your long heavy hair
or the fit of your sex
warm as a cluster of deep summer
days, with wild songs
for each perfect stroke, and a voice,
your voice in my ear
         its incantation.

         For this Anaïs Nin wrote
Little Birds, Gauguin left
Paris for Tahiti,
the hot imprint of a mouth
across skin. For this
we reinvent the world,
slow time upon the pillow,
with kisses impel
each other over the silky
rim of consciousness
         into this rapture.

The Broken World

Impassioned with some song we fail to keep.
—Hart Crane, "The Tunnel"

I'm riding home underground,
"Talk-Net" call-in on my transistor—

pressed to my ear another runaway boy
phoning ratchets of angst

while cigarettes and fatigue tick
and catch in his voice with an engine's

hypnotic whine. The words trip
the car like a golden chain of light

dragged through the heart of this boy
telling the therapist

he's lost his boyfriend to the night's
broken circuitry. An Orphic emptiness

seems to inhabit him, deep exhaustive
breath. There's a distant replica

of myself in his homelessness, a faith
misplaced in leather, even in the flat

admission of rape, how three
older boys forced his body down steps

to a world already broken. If
I hadn't been fifteen

once myself, suspended in an age
where everything you love disappears,

only these eyes would know me, passing under
Times Square, appearing

and dismantling from the panoply
of head shops, gay bars, dirty bookstores.

No place to get lost from other people—
only out-of-body travel

—one good vein after another.
Only these subways that start

then stall then crowd through us,
as I walked out on someone

years ago, believing
the quadrants between revolving

doors a safer reflection.
Or this boy's voice on the radio, rusty

and slick as something
washed from the sea now that he admits

he's no Aphrodite
reeling from improvisation

and gaudy starboys with glittered
eyelids. Some nights I dream

of such a fall, my arms
outstretched, banking like wings,

feet barely touching the cool
concrete borders that tunnel

below the Hudson. Maybe his hustle
is his voice, a dark song hinged

on crackling sparks. Maybe he does sound
too intelligent for the life

he's taken on, his voice as beautiful
as the therapist says.

But I doubt if he could leave the city,
the vicious hands

of boys who fidget for a match,
if amid the frantic simultaneity

he will hold the line a minute more,
not because his parents beat him

or their priest wedged fingers
between his legs as if searching

for the smallest bud of lilac
or wisteria, but because his heart

is as vacant as this train, because
the station lights are winking

and the truth is a cruel and unimportant
thing, because the subway lifts

to gather all the *ruck*
along Columbus Circle

before it crosses *the final level
for the dive.*

The American Dream

In *Viva Las Vegas* it's the scene
where Elvis chases Ann-Margret around
a pool, and she pushes him off
the high-dive. She plays the beautiful
swimming teacher who seduces
a race car driver looking for the perfect
motor, until he catches her
sidelong glances. With wild red hair
she gets what every girl dreams of,

and in a helicopter over Hoover Dam
shows him enough electricity to light
every home for miles. In a sweater and heels
dances the shimmy like no Swede
from Minnesota. They're racing motorcycles
on-screen and off; it's 1964, years
before her fall, the silicone injections
you and your friends will try to match
with Mark Eden Bust Developers.

Watching that scene you squirmed in the dark,
next to a young shoe salesman learned
to love on film what life taught you to hate:
Elvis and Ann-Margret doing the dirty
dog, singing it cheek to cheek
and toe to toe. You swoon to remember
your breast swelling the cup of that salesman's
hand, as if Nevada were the place
where a woman's wish could come true.

Dybbuks

My stepfather swore
she went mad on a train,
watched her mother and sister die
at Birkenau. After the war,
in Brooklyn with her brother
the doctor, she dressed in pearls
and fur, plucked her eyebrows
and penciled them brown.

Every Saturday night
Aunt Sarah phoned us in an accent
of fear, under invented names
as if we were hiding from Nazis.
She was a diabetic protected
by rhinestone glasses, who gift-wrapped
underwear and socks
for Yom Kippur.

To me she was the sarcasm
of a dying neighborhood
who had shed silk
for a loose paisley smock
and though she fed me pounds
of knish, pastrami, and tongue,
she never mentioned
the days in Poland

until one rainy afternoon,
gazing out beveled glass
at cars and trucks
rolling through Flatbush.
I didn't understand then

the catheter whipping
her leg or the five blue numbers
tattooed on a wrist.

I didn't understand either
the little devils she heard
over telephones, the superintendent's
SS armband, how at night
he floated through floors, cut holes
in her linoleum, filled
vacuum cleaner bags
with dirt.

In truth I envied her
secret wound, knowledge of a horror
annihilating the language
of lies, manicured lawns, corduroy
and wool of my youth
or the cockroach that paused
on the drainboard minutes
before her death.

How I wanted to tear sheets
off tables and chairs,
pry nailed windows open and yell
her name across Ocean Avenue,
scatter over wind the bag
of nickels tied at her waist—
her only escape
on the subways of New York.

My Aunt Calls from Bellevue

after Susan Wood

In Bellevue the tunnels wind underground
in a crooked swoon, the way a gypsy woman
sways with her hair full of pins,
and the light is the bulb in a cage.
And if it weren't for the plucking
of piano keys on a distant ward
she'd probably turn toward the toilet,
crouch low in the rank empty darkness,
make herself small. If she could
she'd relive a day in 1939 with her sister
above a street in Lodz, lucky
to have Eva alive. How weightless
she would feel, like leaves
across a courtyard, calling my name.
Instead, we ride the Brighton Beach Line
home from her psychiatrist
while the wind between trains
plays tricks with the dead, the wings
of a pigeon that it raises, suddenly
off a narrow platform. Her legs
are falling asleep with the rhythm,
how easily she could lose her grip
and faint down the pole, how
out of breath when they found her
on a fire escape in Brooklyn, the gas
turned up without lighting the jets.

At night she wakes up to the rasp
of streetcleaners and thinks
their resiny sound is her father's

violin, and she remembers how
her mother worried, fingers
that clutched a sticky chair until
the breaking glass and sirens
ended. Then my aunt takes my arm
in hers. *Sometimes when we dream,*
she says, *time just lifts us out, and we
are saved.* I try to imagine her inside
a paperweight, the ones in which snow
flies when the globe is shaken.
Nothing like this little *wance*
in a housecoat, her face in the first car
pressed against glass. Staring out
at passing stations, she can see
it's only rush hour, the crush
of bodies waiting. And there is
a quickening of the air between us. Next stop
Avenue J, and everywhere the only world
we know is whirling snowflakes,
feverish white.

June Bugs

At dusk she believed their ceaseless drone
  were Messerschmidts raiding the skies of New York.
    From corrugated rainspouts she heard them
whistle fiercely down, cabochon shells ticking
  our stoop on Ocean Avenue. I always tried
    to reassure Aunt Sarah, ran from room to room
shutting off what turned their little motors:
  radio or fan, rotating funnel of electric wind.
    And though it troubles me to compare her
hunched convex back and arms to wings lunging
  toward reflected light, her screams were wrapped
    in lapsing breath. In these moments
nothing could restore her, unless I pretended
  I heard them too, felt the threshing at screens.
    But danger, like beauty, distorts its shape
in rehearsal, meaning fades like starlight
  splayed through curtains, and soon its signals
    cannot be read. Through fog Venus rises,
Orion's pinpoints vanishing over Avenue K,
  over the Ladies of Hadassah, where my aunt knew
    the SS was hiding. Once I watched her
under streetlight, shopping bag and wig,
  gesticulating her warning to anyone walking by,
    each verb pitched like a weight, homesick
for Poland. That was the first time I really looked
  at her, noticed the upward sweep of pain
    in her face as June bugs snapped the air.
I'd forgotten about her chutzpah, the way
  rain lashed at trees in that narrow yard,
    a grief no smile could ever camouflage,

a photograph I saved, the wind of a fan trembling
her Polaroid face between my fingers stirs
those gas-blue eyes slowly back to life.

Geography

for Morton Marcus

This is the geography of a man
who believed in the sadness of place names
unadorned by adjective or verb,
who each morning spread maps
and railroad timetables
over furniture gone wobbly in '29
when he lost his fortune
of railroad bonds, a nobility displaced
in his voice, always this anger
bending to sadness, this cello sound
deep and sonorous as a concerto,
a man who always wore a tie
and detachable collar, 250 pounds
and kept a bar of soap in his shirt drawer,
who smelled sharp and fresh
during a time of no air conditioning
or deodorant, who worked for Wurlitzer Organ
collecting late time payments
at a dime a week, who spent his Depression
pulling electrical wire at Brooklyn
Navy Yard, an Orthodox Jew
who ended up selling pork lard
for Armour Meats, who never touched
money on the Sabbath in front of Gentiles,
who loved Gene Autry westerns, black
and white matinees at the King's Theatre
on Flatbush Avenue, who in 1930
left New York for a day
to marry a woman in a Reformed synagogue

in Knoxville, Tennessee, who labored
in the dim out dark of 1943,
a block warden looking in neighbors' windows
for cracks of light, for blackout
curtains with the rapid impression
of his flashlight, who still rides the Brighton
Beach el, block after combustible block,
his sisters back on cattle cars
to the camps, who opens his eyes
on the passengers who vanish.

Hawthorne Metal, Detroit, 1939

Michelangelo didn't lose any fingers
midnights there, like so many men on hubcap assembly,
jamming sheet metal into punch
press. In the same motion, beating hissing
jaws by seconds and lifting it out,
where any slip of muscle or concentration
would chop down to the knuckle.
With the pulse of small wheels, clank
of wrenches, you could hear him set the broken
jobs, curse beautifully in Italian.

Sundays he'd sleep late under Muscatel
unless the machines at Hawthorne conked,
so bad once the foreman Red, who called
him *wop,* came to dinner. I had to
haul the coal, roll the potato
dumplings and replace the melamine
with Andalucian china
before Mama raised the ancient
pizzalé with boiling
gnocci and angel hair.

Over the rim of a wine glass
Red breathed in the thin sage
of the Carbonieri, and before our seeing-eye Zenith
blubbered at the fate of Don Giovanni,
or lit the ten-cent cigars of a host whose name
ended in a soft vowel, who boasted
the moon was Rome, the sun Detroit.
Into whose grip Red fumbled his limp curled hand
that day, calling him *Mr.*
Cafagña, Mr. Michael *Angelo* Cafagña.

Lady of Guadalupe

Tonight, because Mama died in a public bed, her son Tony's
　　keeping Mr. Taco open late.
So far this place is clean: Canon City, Colorado. His only
　　customer since dinner a hard
wind flouncing awnings over his windows, like her gypsy
　　skirts, no curses left to put
on plates which seem to float like St. Elmo's fire, no dirty
　　glasses to jiggle, the counter
girls all gone home. Only this booth to ponder, the false gold
　　embroidery of vinyl cushions.
He remembers Mama's years stooping over cucumbers
　　in a sun-bleached field outside
Denver, how she hated fermenting the pickles, the stench
　　of vinegar and formaldehyde
rushing fumes into her lungs like something burning,
　　how she hated the job
of standing on rotting platforms stirring foamy pickle vats
　　with a stick, all the dump trucks
from town, that endless green hail of cukes raining
　　down around her churn.
What Tony remembers is the nurse speaking of Mama's heart
　　attack, how she tumbled through
the planks of the boardwalk, how the men lifted her
　　into a low rider, wiped the eyes
rimmed with pickle dust. He remembers the caramel bangs
　　veined with silver, and beautiful
white casket with a reddish-brown center line, how he prayed
　　she'd come back to life
before that cemetery cross, that fat white priest waving
　　a smoking censer over

the raised lid of her coffin, lining embossed with the gold
    medallion Lady of Guadalupe,
and roses pink as Tony's fingers wrenching this mop
    handle over checkered
floors, the ammonia, that pickle smell, or as a boy in Mama's
    hair, loose and lilac
scented. Wishing for this, he scrubs at pots and pans
    as if by polishing
their dull surfaces he could summon her apparition,
    as if the lady might appear.

Working the Spanish Night
of a Ladies Room

after Jimmy Santiago Baca

The door flaps open and the dark maid,
on hands and knees, gathers pearls from a broken string.

Mirrors catch and lose a hundred faces.
Soon the counter will be veiled.

How talc will leave her gazing through patterns
like bromide on glass.

I go back and feel Mamacita, as if a rose
cupping raindrops, her brow lowered in the heat.

Willow Twigs

In Jewish folklore a bunch of hallowed twigs
were used to ward off demons.

—Joshua Sherman

For Sarah Marcus to come home from shopping
    so surprised she'd tiptoe through the examining
        room and find her brother Izzy tied up
naked and dead. For her to flick eyes over
    his rag-stuffed mouth, over the delicacy of thin
        hands she loved like startled birds, palms
opened, bound now together as if in prayer.
    To see the good doctor's face revealed under a row
        of bruises, her sadness shining like tiny buttons
on the smock worn after shock treatments.
    To hear the nurse's voice over the bad connection since
        Izzy'd stopped breathing. Something escaped her.
She didn't sleep anymore but sat up under a sky
    wild with stars and replayed a childhood in Lodz
        where even stormtroopers made wishes
on willow twigs. Souvenirs anyone could wave
    against the cracking dome of night. For her
        nephew to beg that she leave Brooklyn
when Philadelphia was the end of the world.
    Those lives spent in tiny kitchens, for people
        to jump from heights like this, prayer
books open and broken at the spine. To peer
    out unlit windows so she could illuminate the faces
        of her superintendent and his spying Bund
with the Reich, to pad those rooms, silent
    in backless slippers. To listen each night at the rails
        as if she heard the voice of an angel

singing back the names of all the sons
    and fathers lost, or levitate her furniture
        as far down the alphabet of avenues
as she dared, from K to S, to a first floor
    facing the street. For Sarah to kneel in the broken
        glass of the drug cabinet, for the anonymity
of night to suddenly fill her, the way trees
    fill with sparrows in a storm, the way the wind
        changes the color of the sky.

Aunt Sarah (1903–81)

No one wants to celebrate Sukkoth tonight.
    I've come back tired to Brooklyn
up her brownstone steps to hear
    September's fly strum the screen,
to sit where Aunt Sarah sat, lowering
    shades all those mornings
with a diabetic's slow blindness,
    fingernails turning black,
afraid she'll fade like flowered curtains
    in the sun and return
to Auschwitz, a tumor swelling the war
    inside her like a seed.

I want to remember the way leaves fell
    and curled like snapshots
of her brother, how they crumbled
    in her hands like old lace
the day he died. I want to rescue
    a suitcase full of zlotys
from a shuttered room, mourn soup cans
    swollen as corpses, husks
of dead moths on the sill, disembodied
    buttons of coats, needles
crisscrossed like bones, scattered
    below the heavy legs of tables.

I want to resurrect her grief
    each night flung open
like curtains over a fire escape,
    the last light stretched

taut as shirts fluttering wet
    between buildings, women
beating rugs to a sadness long and deep
    as any alley, any penitence
ever paid on Rosh Hashanah so she could
    wrap my sister's breast
like some beautiful Polish doll
    with taffeta and pearls.

Feeding

My aunt liked to slow-boil custard
in a pan, melt the snowy crust,

caramelizing sugar. She beat the yolk,
wooden spoon in a tin ring

until the milk swelled a surface
of liquid and air, as if she could save

the drowned. And she spiked it with whiskey
that none of us could taste,

not even her sister who had drunk
and smoked her way to throat cancer,

her sister who could not swallow any solid
food, only the sweet lava poured in cups

and put before her on a tray.
It touched my aunt to feed someone,

the coagulated cream drawn up
through a straw, her gift of mercy,

slow-boil of custard, morphine, the long
veinlike tube, the human voice

through a tracheostomy, going underwater.

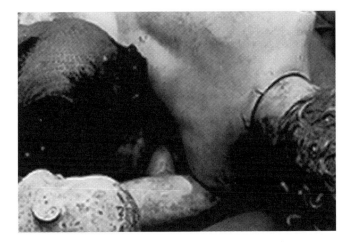

Little Girl in Blue, 1918

The girl in a blue dress is standing
on pink tile and gazing back at the artist
as if looking through him for a place
to rest. The day is brilliant
with Mediterranean light Modigliani fled
for the gravity of dark hotels,
human throats elongated like sunflowers
on the back streets of Paris, barefoot
girls—this girl who glances suggestively
from the corner as if caught in the distance
of another life—who seems about to smile;
and the artist who tugs his brush, wonders
if he can endure TB without cocaine
or brandy, coughing only to palm
the rusty blossom of his chest. The girl
fidgets under plumes of smoke
amid the ashes and empty bottles.
She thinks of trees, how emerald branches
frame her sorrow
and set the cemetery burning
with daffodils. The story
of this path to the studio, the artist who
she understands is dying, how
he's sketched blue walls around her,
how one blank eye looks inward
and the other out toward mercy.

Modigliani: Venus Naturalis

In one of his Venetian nudes, a woman who is twisting her body
in opposite directions
clenches her fists as if extending the moment of orgasm; I longed
for this woman, as a boy
kept her invisible delight like the French postcard that shows
a nymphet reclining

in an Eastern setting, an opium pipe's silken hose wrapping her
wrist with strange
perfume. Nudes were always courtesans, surrounded with detail:
Diana and her forest,
Bathsheba reading a letter, Eve with a view of the garden. Until
Modigliani taught me

to love the working woman, housemaids and waitresses, I did not
love the orchid itself.
There is a peach iridescence, a burnt sienna under his thin coats
of varnish, a hot bath
in which my wife's breasts seem to float, legs and red toenails
pinwheeling her back

to earth. The way ecstasy leaves her hair disheveled and edged
with light, the eyes
weighted under the fatigue of observation, she is like other
Montparnasse characters
he soon will reject, as if she could be possessed by any man,
or by no man at all.

Pornography at Kmart

The artist shops
the DOMESTICS aisle with cringing glances
   for smoked glass to frame her nude
self-portrait. The floorwalker can't take his eyes off
the canvas of a naked woman.
   What strokes his imagination
sends hers back to reformatory, mattress on the floor,
   windows painted black.
Blue light flashes overhead. *Not the usual Kmart fare,*
   she laughs, lifting the painting gingerly.
   Better not be, he snaps—
eyes groping the portrait of a blonde in red sandals,
   transparent voile slip
pulled up around the waist—and blushes at her smile
   in sandy rouge, lipstick mouth
delicate as a gladiola, as the basket of strawberries
   overturned at her feet.
It's always his fetish the mannequin she becomes,
   her skin like polyester spanked
by the static electricity of his hands. And she wonders
   if the smooth sweep of her own blond hair and red
   heels remind him of a boy caught
on a toilet, centerfold crumpled and swirling down
the bowl. His face suddenly a scarlet mask
   like hers before the father
standing with his buckle, before this nightmare
of cashiers in bad ties
tags every desire.

Cracking Eggs

Another 4 A.M. and Dianne stands
staring out the window, staring
through her own reflection
into the dark driveway.
I fidget on the couch,
contemplate the way this house
is chopped into apartments.
Next door the cook has returned home,
drunk again, to his woman and bong.
Both make him cough deep, slam
every door in his two-story apartment:
bedroom door, basement door, cabinet
door, finally the front door
as his woman escapes barefoot
over gravel, bow-legged into the dawn,
bouffant frosted, two hoops
hooked through one lobe. Beer bottles
pop and splinter the driveway
in her absence. Upstairs
the cook belts his punching bag,
fists backfiring like pistons,
an engine running down, Black Sabbath,
REO Speedwagon blasting the thin wall
that separates our lives.
I hold back hard air, clutch my
own fists but wait until we hear it—
his dog, the white German shepherd moaning
low, the dull thud of the beating.
Each night since we moved here like this,
waiting for these college-town cops

who always arrive too late, floodlight
beaming off blue hoods. They inch
out: one male, one female,
dispatch feeding them instructions,
squirming in their belts
before the door of the cook.
The man taps against it politely,
like cracking eggs, afraid
of what he must do.

The Surveyor

He idles a white station wagon
across our road, flicks his door wide
as a switchblade and steps over dirt,
the way hot air escapes the surface

of the earth, the edge of wetlands
even this rainless spring can't
lift. My wife knows what's
coming: Christmas Tree Village.

She spits out seeds as watermelon
runs between our feet, newspaper's
classified section wet
as dead skin against the porch.

Then swiping her fingers across
her jeans she's gone inside,
screen slapping while I fish
a smoke, shake out the match,

its tiny blue tail curling
in the heat. And sure enough,
the surveyor aims his tripod,
drums clipboard with mechanical

pencil as if he's grown impatient
with the pines, the wild grass,
the standing swamp that was
Lake Lansing. When suddenly

from this dream of backfill, boon
of condos, multicomplex living—
all of it lost for moments
down that sinkhole of mind—

a blackbird screams and before
his work the surveyor pauses
as if he might reconsider, as if
red wings could wake him.

Mammography

Kleenex in your fist
sunflower of hair,
eyes bright as tourmaline,
paisley gown replacing your
dress, white tag
for a bracelet.

That morning in the waiting
room I hunched over
teakwood, heart drumming
against a revelry of purple
carpeting and game shows,
the clicking, rattling, ringing
of ordinary things, the useless
eyes of other patients
and their families.

A nurse whisked in
calling my name. I struggled open
a heavy door and followed
the shoes of that woman
through a clean narrow corridor.

I pulled a chair as close
to yours as two chairs
can go, and held you from there
while the nurse popped the TV on.
And we gazed into it:
the green-tinted shower
of a green-tinted woman
touching breasts with her hands
so any woman might learn
her cancer.

When the nurse returned
with X rays in hand,
no lumps but
the lump
in my throat.

All the Bells

All the bells say: too late.
—John Berryman, *The Dream Songs*, 29

1
It starts with your wish
that we end our lives
with gas or gun or pills.

2
So many nights you couldn't sleep
thoughts circled your head
and dark air carried
you back to being
a young mother, an ex-wife, a chatterbox
on the gallows.
                    Barely conscious
in the dark, the bruises on a body
no one touched, the longing
for death no one soothed, the black
wings wound about your skull.

3
At the highway's edge we've learned
to time our lives by the ebb and flow
of traffic, engine heat surfacing the boundary
of a porch where once you graded
papers. Standing beneath the moon's milky drag
I knew this would all disappear
like endless rows of faces pressed
at passing windows, our shelves and pictures
trembled with the bass notes of cars.
The news made me imagine a car

ganged with men, your yellow hair
a rope, and fists clenched
tight as buds, as if the sea
of white noise rising off the road
had finally lulled you
underwater. Just as watching you sleep
I fought a husband's urge to wake you
from this world to the next.

4

When I found you that morning,
head turned in the noose,
I couldn't believe you had died, couldn't
believe in the ruin of your throat
or lips, ripe as a peach orchard
pear. When I think of you now
I see you hanging so limp from the rafter,
the white extension cord coiled
around your neck, tongue bulging
between your teeth, bare feet floating
in mid-air, body stiff with a kind of flight.

5

How furiously I tried to breathe
and pump what breath there was
back into your chest, back
into the futile shell of the body,
unable to distinguish that small wind
from the thin rattle
of bracelets, golden rings
like eyes across our dresser.

6

When the medics arrived, I prayed
you were not dead, prayed for the machinery,

the breathing harness. I was lost
in the living room while a clean-shaven cop
muscled me toward a calm
I could not understand. I have seen terrors
but never so sudden an instant of time
wild as the prick of a needle,
the TV running senselessly, as I ran
from room to room, and down
steps for you, to a basement
where your body dangled.

7
When I drive past our old brick townhouse
I see them—red and yellow—
the tulips you planted last spring
risen from the ground after winter.

8
The blurred figure of the body rests
its psychic life, where the smallest cone
of incense burning in a bowl offers up
spiraled arms. I thought what we needed
was a newspaper, a greasy bag of donuts
on the Halloween Sunday
morning I found you gone.

9
You must unravel your noose, unleash it
from your collar bone, sing
a sweet breath choking.
Let it surge out, let it down
like a bolt of hair, let its braided knot
untangle, let it unwind
like pearls—release it; the ivory
curves of your shoulders shining, your skin triumphant—

let it shame the hangman. You must unravel
your noose, tear it from your throat,
a song of what's been bruised
and cracked by the blue dislocation
of your spine, like pearls
the cords of your beautiful neck,
taut thin shadow
on your face looking up.

The Impossible Line

for Dianne Cafagña, 1949–93

I weigh the hearts that vanish
by degrees, against the boards
which have so sadly creaked
beneath this woman—the child
who found her friend hanging in an orchard
of apples and bright red scarfs,
of apples and bright red scarfs and knots—
who is willing to risk love
by the shimmering fit of a dress,
by the whiskey on her breath tinged
with the sweet residue of bitterness
but ripe as Indian summer.
So dangerous tonight, and slinky
in her red silk
that wetting my lips, I can taste
the tumble of blonde fire
when we touch, scattering
a pale-gold necklace of scent,
the leaves, the fragrance
of a tree. The heat of her hand
on my spine like a current,
closing my eyes, moving me
against her, blind, when I look
back at old lovers' faces,
at what I've often thought was
pity, which disappears like shadows
or a wish that couldn't save them,
our words gone like sparks burned up
in darkness, walking late at night alone

with only our coats to button
and gather our warmth about us.
And through her empty rooms long silences murmur
the echo of fields, these slow dances
that hold us close, her back
which follows an impossible line.

Back in the World

The days are dry and cool now,
the wind in the trees moving birds
over branches, things we've left behind
gathered suddenly to the couch,
our cat hunched between us.
Except at night when no one's watching
and we return to this room,
stand with our longing and forget
easy intention, forget the world
going on without us, find our way through
the tapestry of music trees make
with cars out on the road. This humming
just a tease, the way my wife flips
the pages of a book before she bursts
and pauses with a soulful look,
the beautiful insistence
that we meet again like each star
turned to join the twilight.

Poems from the Sangamon
John Knoepfle (1985)

In It
Stephen Berg (1986)

The Ghosts of Who We Were
Phyllis Thompson (1986)

Moon in a Mason Jar
Robert Wrigley (1986)

Lower-Class Heresy
T. R. Hummer (1987)

Poems: New and Selected
Frederick Morgan (1987)

Furnace Harbor: A Rhapsody of the
North Country
Philip D. Church (1988)

Bad Girl, with Hawk
Nance Van Winckel (1988)

Blue Tango
Michael Van Walleghen (1989)

Eden
Dennis Schmitz (1989)

Waiting for Poppa at the Smithtown
Diner
Peter Serchuk (1990)

Great Blue
Brendan Galvin (1990)

What My Father Believed
Robert Wrigley (1991)

Something Grazes Our Hair
S. J. Marks (1991)

Walking the Blind Dog
G. E. Murray (1992)

The Sawdust War
Jim Barnes (1992)

The God of Indeterminacy
Sandra McPherson (1993)

Off-Season at the Edge of the World
Debora Greger (1994)

Counting the Black Angels
Len Roberts (1994)

Oblivion
Stephen Berg (1995)

To Us, All Flowers Are Roses
Lorna Goodison (1995)

Honorable Amendments
Michael S. Harper (1995)

Points of Departure
Miller Williams (1995)

Dance Script with Electric Ballerina
Alice Fulton (reissue, 1996)

To the Bone: New and Selected
Poems
Sydney Lea (1996)

Floating on Solitude
Dave Smith (3-volume reissue, 1996)

Bruised Paradise
Kevin Stein (1996)

Walt Whitman Bathing
David Wagoner (1996)

National Poetry Series

Eroding Witness
Nathaniel Mackey (1985)
Selected by Michael S. Harper

Palladium
Alice Fulton (1986)
Selected by Mark Strand

Cities in Motion
Sylvia Moss (1987)
Selected by Derek Walcott

The Hand of God and a Few
Bright Flowers
William Olsen (1988)
Selected by David Wagoner

The Great Bird of Love
Paul Zimmer (1989)
Selected by William Stafford

Stubborn
Roland Flint (1990)
Selected by Dave Smith

The Surface
Laura Mullen (1991)
Selected by C. K. Williams

The Dig
Lynn Emanuel (1992)
Selected by Gerald Stern

My Alexandria
Mark Doty (1993)
Selected by Philip Levine

The High Road to Taos
Martin Edmunds (1994)
Selected by Donald Hall

Theater of Animals
Samn Stockwell (1995)
Selected by Louise Glück

The Broken World
Marcus Cafagña (1996)
Selected by Yusef Komunyakaa

Her Soul beneath the Bone:
Women's Poetry on Breast Cancer
Edited by Leatrice Lifshitz (1988)

Days from a Dream Almanac
Dennis Tedlock (1990)

Working Classics: Poems on
Industrial Life
*Edited by Peter Oresick and
Nicholas Coles* (1990)

Hummers, Knucklers, and Slow
Curves: Contemporary Baseball
Poems
Edited by Don Johnson (1991)

The Double Reckoning of
Christopher Columbus
Barbara Helfgott Hyett (1992)

Selected Poems
Jean Garrigue (1992)

New and Selected Poems, 1962–92
Laurence Lieberman (1993)

The Dig *and* Hotel Fiesta
Lynn Emanuel (1994)

For a Living: The Poetry of Work
*Edited by Nicholas Coles and Peter
Oresick* (1995)

The Tracks We Leave: Poems on
Endangered Wildlife of North
America
Barbara Helfgott Hyett (1996)

Other Poetry Volumes

Local Men *and* Domains
James Whitehead (1987)